MOMENTS OF TRUTH

VOLUME I

VOLUME I

MOMENTS
OF TRUTH

❖

Excerpts from

The Rubaiyat of Omar Khayyam
EXPLAINED

by Paramhansa Yogananda

CRYSTAL CLARITY, PUBLISHERS
Nevada City, California

Hardbound edition, first printing 1995

Copyright © J. Donald Walters

All rights reserved
ISBN 1-56589-721-8
10 9 8 7 6 5 4 3 2 1

Designed by Christine Schuppe
Illustrated by Sarah Moffatt

Printed in Hong Kong

CRYSTAL
CLARITY
PUBLISHERS

14618 Tyler Foote Road, Nevada City, California 95959
1-800-424-1055

Introduction

THIS BOOK CONTAINS nuggets of wisdom excerpted from one of the great works of modern times: *The Rubaiyat of Omar Khayyam Explained,* by Paramhansa Yogananda. The excerpts here contained are not from the poem itself, but from the commentary. They are words to live by: wise insights by one of the great spiritual figures of our times that have the power profoundly to change people's lives.

As Yogananda explains in *The Rubaiyat . . . Explained,* Omar Khayyam's work is deeply spiritual; it is not, as most Westerners believe, a poem in praise of earthly pleasures. Taking the inner meaning of this work to ever greater depths, Paramhansa Yogananda produced one of his own deepest and most profoundly moving spiritual works.

— J. Donald Walters, Editor

God is Eternal Silence.
To those who
love Him purely
He speaks
through the voice
of silent intuition.

Stanza 6

Waste not these few,
precious earth years.
The bird of life
has but a short arc
of time to fly.
Soon — ah,
how sadly soon! —
it will slip its earthly form
and vanish
into the Infinite.

Stanza Seven

O discerning one!
rise above life's dualities,
above the endless gradations
of relativity.
Lo! every plan for success,
so wantonly embraced;
every looming disaster,
so fearfully denied —
all have as their sum total: zero!
What are they but fictions —
fleeting mind-children
in life's constantly
changing dream?
Ignore them!

Stanza Nine

Let the world shout in outrage,
or leap up and down
in a hysteria of false joy.
What matters it?
It is all a parade —
entertaining, colorful,
but for all that
only a parade,
passing endlessly.

Stanza Nine

People everywhere,
in their quest for
happiness outside themselves,
discover in the end
that they've been seeking it
in an empty cornucopia,
and sucking feverishly
at the rim of a crystal glass
into which was never poured
the wine of joy.

Stanza Ten

Happiness blooms naturally
in the hearts
of those who are
inwardly free.
It flows spontaneously,
like a mountain spring
after April showers,
in minds that are contented
with simple living
and that willingly renounce
the clutter of unnecessary,
so-called "necessities" —
the dream castles of a
restless mind.

Stanza Eleven

To seek happiness
outside ourselves
is like trying to
lasso a cloud.
Happiness is not a thing:
It is a state of mind.
It must be *lived*.

Stanza Twelve

"Look within,"
whispers the rose.
"Open your consciousness
to soul-understanding,
ere the petals of your life
fall and scatter
on the garden path —
lovely no longer,
but shriveled, lifeless —
brown."

Stanza Thirteen

The only worthwhile
accomplishments
are not those
we achieve outwardly,
but the victories
we win over ourselves.

Stanza Seventeen

Every thought we think
is a flower in life's garden,
and not the permanent
possession of anyone.
Let our thoughts, then,
be fragrant and beautiful,
not rank and ugly,
that the memory we leave
behind us
be felt as a blessing
on the earth.

Stanza Eighteen

If you succeed in finding
happiness in your soul,
then even though
you die tomorrow
and join the long procession
of departed souls
that slowly moves down
pillared corridors of centuries,
you will always carry with you
that priceless treasure.

Stanza Twenty

In daily meditation,
penetrate the veil of the senses;
pass beyond them
to the soul-peace within.
In the temple of inner silence
you will find proof positive
of God's existence.

Stanza Twenty-Six

As long as we continue to dwell,
as uncounted millions do,
in a welter of desires,
restless and unstable,
we remain earth-bound:
confined like rivers between
high embankments
of matter-consciousness.

Stanza Twenty-Eight

Behold this one flaming truth:
All life is fleeting.
Cling to that understanding,
and seek, then,
within yourself
that which alone endures.

Stanza Twenty-Six

The body is
a temporary stopping place.
Beyond it,
tracks lead in two directions
into the unknown:
toward death,
if that be your choice;
or to a life
of immortality
in God.

Stanza Three

The real purpose
for your earthly sojourn
is to quaff deeply the nectar
of reincarnation-destroying,
all-misery-annihilating wisdom.

Fill your consciousness
with true, lasting happiness.
Lo! all too soon
life's vitality will evaporate
from its little cup of flesh,
and vanish forever
into the mysterious unknown.

Stanzas Two and Three

Be neither
elated nor depressed
at anything outside yourself.
Behold the passing
spectacle of life
with an even mind.
For life's ups and downs
are but waves on an ocean,
constantly in flux.
Shun emotional involvement with them,
while remaining ever calm,
ever happy at your inner center
in the spine.

Stanza Nine

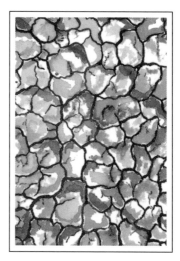

How foolish the worldly man,
to identify his immortal soul
with something that, at death,
becomes mere clay,
barren of any vestige
of beauty!

Stanza Fifteen

Please send me more information about . . .

☐ **Other books, tapes, and videos** from *Crystal Clarity, Publishers*

☐ **Free Sample Lesson** of the *Fourteen Steps*, a home study course on meditation and yoga

☐ **Retreats and Programs** at *The Expanding Light*, Ananda's internationally known retreat

☐ **Seminars** on the subject of this book or related topics

. . . or call 1-800-424-1055

Name _____

Address _____

City _____ State _____ Zip _____

Phone _____

Crystal Clarity, Publishers
14618 Tyler Foote Rd.
Nevada City, CA 95959

Live *behind* the scenes
of relative time,
in the unchanging present.
Only by living properly
right now,
at the changeless center
of the moment,
can we arrive at that point
where we exercise
complete control
over our lives.

Stanza Thirty-Seven

The end result
of emotional extremes
is extreme emotional
dissatisfaction.
Perfect happiness lies not
at any of the extremities
of outer experiences,
but at a point of calmness
midway between them all.

Stanza Thirty-Nine

As you travel steadfastly
along the path
of inner peace,
avoid exciting yourself
over outward events
in your life.
Do not take things
too seriously:
They will be what they will be.
Life pursues
its own tortuous paths,
forever unpredictably.

Stanza Forty-Five

Let not your possessions
possess *you*,
nor the petty details
of worldly life
invade with hordes of worry
the stillness of your heart.

Stanza Forty-Two

The black squares on a checkerboard
alternate with the white.
Even so, every darkness in life
alternates with light,
every sorrow with a joy,
every failure with a success.
Change and contrast
are inevitable,
and are what make
the great game possible.
View them dispassionately,
and never allow them
to define who you are, inside.

Stanza Forty-Nine

The more we live
guided from within,
the greater our control
over outer events
in the great game of life.
For when we live
at our own center,
in superconsciousness,
we live in the only
true freedom there is.

Stanza Fifty

Even one contact
with God in meditation
fills the soul
with bliss and wisdom
far beyond the pallid hope
tendered by priests
through ritual and
learned discourse.

Stanza Fifty-Six

What a travesty of religion!
to allow the sweetness
of inner silence
to be drowned
in the clang and hubbub
of temple lectures,
theologians' arguments,
and noisy rituals.

Stanza Fifty-Six

Every soul
was given free will
at the start of its long,
winding journey
through time.

Stanza Sixty

At the heart of every atom
there dwells the
divine impulse —
the impulse to
transform selfhood
into Infinite Spirit.

Stanza Sixty-One

Perfection can be attained
only by attuning
one's actions
to inner,
soul-guidance.

Stanza Sixty

Evolution is an ever clearer,
ever more overt
manifestation of divine
consciousness.

Stanza Sixty-One

Consciousness
did not appear temporarily
out of unconsciousness,
for everything
in the universe
is an expression of
consciousness.

Stanza Sixty-One

In the rocks and soil, God sleeps.
In the plants, God projects gentle movement.

In the flowers, God suggests to our minds
His infinite beauty.
In the flowers and blossoms,
with their fragrance and their colorful quilts
of petals, God smiles invitingly,
as if to tell us, "Remember Me."

In the birds and animals,
God projects consciousness as activity.

In mankind, physical evolution
attains its highest development.

Stanza Sixty-One

He who made us
must surely also love us.
His reason for ordaining death
as the final act of life
must, therefore,
be somehow connected
with His love.

Stanza Sixty-Two

God feels no anger,
no matter
how many times we err.
He is the Fountainhead
of limitless,
unconditional love.

Stanza Sixty-Two

One who was born
disadvantaged in any way
should resist fiercely
the temptation
to wallow in self-pity.
To feel sorry for oneself
is to dilute
one's inner power
to overcome.

Stanza Sixty-Three

There are *no* obstacles:
There are only
opportunities!

Stanza Sixty-Three

The ordinary man
considers himself
the hammered-out product
of circumstances,
rather than
their creator.

Stanza Sixty-Five

As a man allows himself
to depend increasingly
on circumstances
outside himself
for his physical, mental,
and spiritual nourishment,
never looking within
to his own source,
he gradually depletes
his reserves of energy.

Stanza Sixty-Five

Worldly consciousness
is a dark, brooding land,
perilous with the shadows
of fear and death.

Stanza Sixty-Eight

Fly no longer
in aimless circles
above the shores
of death.
Drunk with ecstasy,
and borne aloft
on divine bliss-currents,
fly onward
with steady wing-beats
to the distant shores
of immortality.

Stanza Seven

Ah, what joy awaits you
in the drumbeat of
Infinity —
distant-seeming,
yet never farther away
than your own
inner power to hear!

Stanza Twelve

Sacred peace flows,
sap-like, within the spine,
the tree of Life.
As you relax there,
breathe deeply the pure, fresh,
revivifying atmosphere;
drink the intoxicating wine
of spiritual bliss.

Stanza Eleven

Intelligence
should not be confused
with wisdom.
There are many
highly intelligent
fools in the world,
who use their intellects
to justify,
not to eliminate,
their delusion.

Stanza Thirty-Three

The most notable difference
between being "down-to-earth" spiritually,
and being "down-to-earth" in a worldly sense,
is that spiritual realism is expansive,
whereas worldly realism
is usually contractive.

Spiritual realism — the willingness,
for example, to face uncompromisingly
the full truth about oneself —
softens the heart and fills it eventually
with kindness toward all.
Worldly realism, on the other hand,
too often hardens the heart,
filling it with pride and selfishness.

Stanza Thirty-One

Without God,
human love is never perfect.
No marriage is truly fruitful
without the "secret ingredient"
of divine love.
Earthly love
that reaches not past the beloved
to embrace divinity
is not real love at all.
It is ego-worship,
selfish because rooted
in desire.

Stanza Thirty-Two

To the worldly man,
the body seems
made of "clay."
To the spiritual master,
it is a manifestation
of pure Spirit.

Stanza Sixty-One

Work diligently
to replace evil habits
with wholesome,
God-reminding ones.
Be introspective,
ever watchful,
ready in a moment
to banish the tramp,
temptation,
if he tries to enter
the polished sanctuary
of your self-control.

Stanza Seventy

We can awake
from this dream of life
only by making it
a reflection of truth.
We cannot dismiss it
by merely calling it unreal.
Though dreaming
this appearance of reality,
we have to eat, sleep,
earn our living,
and struggle in the face
of karmic challenges.
So why not dream victory?

Stanza Forty-Six

Time, for us, passes
in almost dreamlike sequences,
like images seen
through undulating
ocean currents.
Yesterday's "realities"
are already a bit faded —
like carpets
after being left
in the sun.

Stanza Forty-Six

Significant
achievements in life
are never made
except by people
who are willing to forego
popular approval
in their quest for goals
which their hearts tell them
are right and true.

Stanza Seventy-Two

The worldly person's
sense of honor
rests shakily
on the good opinion
of others,
most of whom
are as deluded as himself!

Stanza Sixty-Nine

Blame no one
for the evils that beset you.
Accept responsibility
for your own life, and
for whatever misfortunes
you encounter.

Stanza Fifty-Seven

For spiritual development,
inner strength is necessary.
Spiritual development
is not for weaklings.

Stanza Fifty-Eight

Intellectuality
cannot produce the
sturdy oak of wisdom.
Only spare tumbleweed
of shallow thoughts
can survive in the
dry desert of
matter-consciousness.

Stanza Fifty-Five

Break the bars
of detail-consciousness.
Don't interrupt
life's natural flow by
damming its river
at every bend
with brittle sticks of
analysis and definition.

Stanza Forty-One

The longer one can enjoy
the peaceful after-effects
of meditation,
the more quickly
he will develop intuition.

Stanza Fifty-Nine

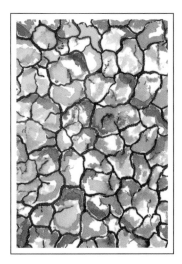

No matter how dry,
clay-hard, and cracked
the soil of your heart
has become
during famine years
of sense-indulgence,
of failure and disappointment,
it can be watered
and softened again
by peace-showers
of inner communion.

Stanza Sixty-five

Life could have been
so beautiful,
had mankind only lived
as God intended.
Instead, human life
has become a jumble box
to hold the pieces
of a mad jigsaw puzzle —
a confusing assortment
of evil and good,
sorrow and joy,
death and life.

Stanza Seventy-Three

Happiness itself, though a universal good,
must never be imposed on others;
in fact, it never can be.
When a diamond cutter wants
to produce a beautiful stone,
he knows that he must cut it
along its natural cleavage.
His cut must not be random,
to satisfy some abstract fancy of his own.
The same is true for bringing out
the beauty in human nature:
We must take into account
the realities of others,
and never seek
to impose on them our own.

Stanza Seventy-Three

The nerves are channels through which
the life-force enables the mind and body to interact.
As the life-force moves down the spine
and out to the body and its senses,
the mind is drawn outward also.
Sense-stimulation from within
impels one to seek fulfillment in sense-pleasures.

This same nervous system, however, constitutes
the one and only path to spiritual enlightenment,
regardless of a person's formal religious affiliation.
When the energy can be coaxed to reverse its flow
from the senses to the brain,
it reveals to our consciousness another world.

With progressive interiorization,
through daily meditation,
one develops subtle, inner perceptions
vastly more satisfying than
their muted echoes from the senses.

Stanza Thirty-One

Autobiography of a Yogi by Paramhansa Yogananda. The original 1946 edition of the classic spiritual autobiography, which relates the life of Yogananda, the first yoga master of India whose mission it was to live and teach in the West. This book has helped launch, and continues to inspire, a spiritual awakening throughout the Western world.

The Rubaiyat of Omar Khayyam Explained by Paramhansa Yogananda. Nearly 50 years ago Yogananda discovered a scripture previously unknown to the world. It was hidden in the beautiful, sensual imagery of the beloved poem, *The Rubaiyat of Omar Khayyam*. His commentary reveals the spiritual mystery behind this world-famous love poem. Long considered as a celebration of earthly pleasure, now *The Rubaiyat* is revealed to be a profound spiritual teaching.

The Essence of Self-Realization A remarkable collection of never-before-published quotations by Paramhansa Yogananda. It offers as complete an explanation of life's true purpose, and of the way to achieve that purpose, as may be found anywhere. Compiled by J. Donald Walters.

Other Selections

The Path: A Spiritual Autobiography by J. Donald Walters. The moving story of Mr. Walters's search for meaning, and its fulfillment during his years of training under Paramhansa Yogananda. In over 400 stories and sayings of Yogananda, the reader is given an inspiring glimpse into what it was like to live with one of the great masters of modern times.

Rays of the Same Light Parallel passages from the Bible and the Bhagavad Gita, with commentary by J. Donald Walters. *Rays* probes the underlying similarities between these two great scriptures, and presents deep mystical teaching blended with practical common sense.

How to Meditate A concise, step-by-step guide to the timeless art and science of meditation. Written by John Novak, who has studied, practiced, and taught meditation for over 25 years.

Yoga Postures for Higher Awareness A unique approach by J. Donald Walters, emphasizing the mental and spiritual benefits, as well as the physical.

Affirmations for Self-Healing A collection of fifty-two spiritual qualities and a discussion of each, with an affirmation and prayer for its realization. Written by J. Donald Walters.

The "Secrets" Series
by J. Donald Walters
A thought for each day of the month

Secrets of Love
Secrets of Happiness
Secrets of Friendship
Secrets of Inner Peace
Secrets of Marriage
Secrets of Success
Secrets for Men
Secrets for Women
Secrets of Prosperity
Secrets of Leadership
Secrets of Self-Acceptance
Secrets of Winning People
Secrets of Meditation
Secrets of Radiant Health and Well-Being
Secrets of Emotional Healing
Secrets of Bringing Peace on Earth
Life's Little Secrets *(for children)*
Little Secrets of Success *(for children)*
Little Secrets of Happiness *(for children)*
Little Secrets of Friendship *(for children)*

For information about these or other
Crystal Clarity products call:
1-800-424-1055

CRYSTAL CLARITY
A new concept in living

Crystal Clarity means to see oneself, and all things, as aspects of a greater reality; to seek to enter into conscious attunement with that reality; and to see all things as channels for the expression of that reality.

It means to see truth in simplicity; to seek always to be guided by the simple truth, not by opinion; and by what *is*, not by one's own desires or prejudices.

It means striving to see things in relation to their broadest potential.

In one's association with other people, it means seeking always to include their realities in one's own.